Mental Training for Soccer

Pre-teens & Teens Edition

Maria C. Bruce

ISBN: 9798320192727

Acknowledgements

MANY THANKS TO

My husband Eric, who has always encouraged me to follow my passions, and whose support has always kept me moving forward.

My son Nico, my inspiration for this book, and whose feedback has been key to making this book happen.

My daughter Vicky, who has been my cheerleader and always pushes me to do more.

My parents, Freddy and Elsa, and my sister, Ceci, who have always supported and believed in me.

MENTAL TRAINING FOR SOCCER

Pre-teens & Teens Edition

Chapter 1
Understanding Your Mind - The Soccer Player's Secret Weapon

The Importance of your Mind in Soccer

Let's kick off with a question: what makes a great soccer player? You might think of excellent ball handling, lightning-fast speed, or a killer instinct for finding the back of the net. Sure, all these attributes are important, but there's another ingredient, often overlooked, that truly separates the good from the great. It's the mind!

Just like your legs, your lungs, or your heart, your mind is a muscle. And like any muscle, it needs to be trained and conditioned to perform at its best. So let's explore the power of your mind and how it relates to soccer skills.

Think of your favorite soccer player. Let's say, for example, Lionel Messi. He makes dribbling past defenders look like a walk in the park, right? That's because Messi has spent countless hours practicing those moves. But, more importantly, he's spent equal, if not more time, training his mind to make split-second decisions and handle the pressure of the game.

Understanding your mind is about knowing your strengths and weaknesses, acknowledging your fears, harnessing your focus, and learning to see challenges as opportunities to grow. The first step to understanding your mind is to recognize that it has a massive impact on your performance, both on and off the field.

You might be wondering, "How does my mind affect my soccer skills?" Well, consider this - have you ever missed a penalty and then couldn't stop thinking about it for the rest of the game? That's your mind in action!

Your mind can be your biggest cheerleader or your toughest opponent. It can lift you up when you're down, or it can fill you with self-doubt at the crucial moment. The good news? You are in control. You can train your mind to be positive, resilient, and focused, just like Messi, or any of your soccer heroes.

Now, understanding your mind is not a one-time thing. It's a journey, a process. It's like learning to dribble or shoot. The more you practice, the better you'll get at it. In the next chapters, we'll explore how to embrace a growth mindset and grit, the power of visualization, relaxation and focus techniques, and how to reframe negative thoughts. But first, let's understand how the brain and mind works a little more.

HOW THE BRAIN AND MIND WORKS

When you see your favorite player executing a flawless free kick or making a spectacular save, you're not just witnessing physical skills. You're also seeing mental strength in action. Every decision in soccer, whether to pass, shoot, or defend, is made in the mind before it's executed on the field.

Your brain is like a supercomputer that controls everything you do, think, and feel. It's the command center of your body and mind. Just like a muscle, the more you exercise and challenge your brain, the stronger and smarter it becomes. But how does it learn?

When you learn something new, like a new soccer skill, your brain creates connections between different neurons. These connections are pathways that allow information to travel and form memories. The more you practice and repeat a skill, the stronger these connections become. This process is called neuroplasticity, and it's what allows you to improve and master new abilities.

Going a little deeper into this process, when you're learning a new move or technique, your brain goes through a series of steps to help you master it:

Step 1: **Observation** - Your brain takes in information by watching and paying attention to skilled players or coaches. It analyzes their movements and processes the visual input.

Step 2: **Visualization** - Before you even try the skill, your brain can mentally rehearse it. This helps activate the same neural pathways that would be used during actual execution.

Step 3: **Execution** - When you attempt the skill, your brain sends signals to your muscles, coordinating their movements to perform the desired action. This is where practice and repetition play a crucial role.

Step 4: **Feedback** - Your brain receives feedback from your body and the environment (for example, your coaches). It uses this information to adjust and refine your movements, making them more accurate and efficient.

USING YOUR WORDS AND THOUGHTS TO TRAIN YOUR MIND

Picture this: you're standing on the field with the ball at your feet, surrounded by opponents. In that moment, what you say to yourself and the thoughts that run through your mind can make a world of difference. Our words and thoughts have a direct influence on our body's response. By consciously filling our minds with positive thoughts and visualizing success, we can build confidence, focus, and resilience. So, when faced with challenges, instead of doubting yourself, repeat empowering phrases like "I am capable," "I can do this," or "I am a skilled player." Embracing this positive self-talk will help you stay motivated and perform at your best.

⚽ Activity: Training positive thoughts and self-talk.

1. Create a list of positive thoughts related to soccer and your personal goals. You can use the examples below as inspiration, or choose your own sentences. Write down the ones that resonate with you the most to keep your mind positive and remind yourself of your strengths and goals.

Some Positive Thoughts examples:

1. I am a skilled soccer player and I believe in my abilities.

2. I am dedicated to improving my soccer skills and becoming even better.

3. I embrace challenges and use them to grow stronger and more confident.

4. I am resilient and bounce back from setbacks with determination.

5. I am an important member of my team, and I contribute to our success.

6. I am focused and fully present in each game and practice.

7. I have the power to overcome any obstacles that come my way.

8. I am confident in my decision-making and trust my instincts on the field.

9. I am disciplined and committed to giving my best effort in every training session.

10. I am a positive influence on my teammates and support them both on and off the field.

_____

_____

_____

_____

_____

_____

_____

_____

_____

⚽ Activity: Goal Setting

1. Write down your goals in soccer, both short-term and long-term. Try to be specific and realistic when describing your goals.

_____

_____

_____

_____

_____

_____

_____

_____

_____

_____

2. Think back to when you started playing, and reflect on your progress so far. Write down any improvements you've made, and also areas where you still need work. This activity will help you develop a growth mindset by emphasizing the importance of constant improvement and celebrating small victories along the way.

_____

_____

_____

_____

Chapter 2
Growth Mindset and Grit in Soccer

Unleashing the Power of Growth Mindset

In soccer, having a growth mindset is like having a secret weapon on the field. It's all about believing that your skills and abilities can be developed through practice and hard work. Instead of seeing mistakes and setbacks as failures, you see them as opportunities to learn, grow, and be a better player.

Imagine you're facing a tough team who seems unbeatable. A player with a growth mindset would view this challenge as a chance to improve his skills and tactics. He would embrace the opportunity to learn from the experience, analyze his performance, and come back even stronger next time. On the other hand, a player with a fixed mindset might get discouraged and believe that he'll never be able to compete at that level.

The good news is that even if you have a fixed mindset, **you can train your mind to start thinking in a positive way.** To develop a growth mindset in soccer, remember that every practice, every game, and every setback is a chance to improve. Embrace challenges, be open and seek feedback from coaches and teammates, and believe in your ability to continuously grow as a player. With a growth mindset, there's no limit to how far you can go in the world of soccer.

THE DETERMINATION OF GRIT ON THE PITCH

Now, let's talk about grit—that is, the determination and perseverance that fuels you while playing soccer. Grit is one of the things that separates good players from great players. It's the willingness to put in the extra hours of practice (even in bad weather!), to push through fatigue during a tough game, and to never give up even when the odds are against you.

Think about a time when you faced a setback in soccer—a missed goal, a defeat, or an injury. How did you respond?

Did you let it discourage you, or did you find the inner strength to keep going? Gritty players view setbacks as temporary obstacles, not a permanent defeat. **They use failures as fuel to improve and come back stronger.**

Again, the good news is that grit can also be developed and grown. The key is to focus on your long-term goals and stay committed to them. Set small, achievable targets along the way and celebrate each milestone reached - for example, if you finally made that goal in the top corner angle, celebrate it by telling your friends and family. When faced with challenges, remind yourself how much you enjoy playing the game, and how happy you feel after a fun match. Stay determined, stay focused, and keep pushing forward, no matter what.

GROWTH MINDSET & GRIT

By adopting a **growth mindset**, you can unlock your full potential as a player and continuously improve. With **grit**, you can overcome any obstacle on the field and persevere until you achieve greatness.

⚽ Activity: Growth Mindset Exercise - Learning from Role Models

1. Choose a professional soccer player whom you admire and consider successful.
2. Research and gather information about their background, career, and notable achievements.
3. Write a paragraph about their key qualities or mindset that have contributed to their success. Identify specific examples or stories that demonstrate their growth mindset.
4. Reflect on how you can incorporate those qualities or mindset into your own soccer journey.

Example:

1. Role Model: Lionel Messi
2. Lionel Messi is one of the greatest soccer players of all time. As a kid, he endured leaving his family and friends behind, to move abroad and have a better chance of becoming a professional soccer player. He also overcame many difficult years of treatment for growth hormone deficiency, but his determination and love for soccer kept him going.
3. He always trained hard, and focused on his ultimate goal: winning the world cup. After failures and disappointments with his National team, his growth mindset allowed him to stay focused, and keep

believing he would achieve his goal. His hard work and strong mind ultimately paid off, which was celebrated by Messi personally, and by millions of fans around the world.

4. To achieve a similar mindset, I can start by setting specific goals for different aspects of my game (example, I will visualize scoring a perfect goal, before shooting a free kick). I will see challenges as opportunities for growth rather than obstacles (example, the opponent dribbled past me, what can I do differently to stop him next time). By working hard on practices, taking feedback from my coach, and staying persistent, I can build up a growth mindset and keep improving my soccer skills.

_____

_____

_____

_____

_____

_____

_____

_____

_____

_____

_____

⚽ ACTIVITY: MISTAKE ANALYSIS TO DEVELOP GROWTH MINDSET

Mistakes are an inevitable part of learning and growth. Let's work on finding the positives even when practice, or the game, were not what you hoped. This activity will help you develop a growth mindset, by teaching you to see mistakes as opportunities for learning and improvement, rather than as failures.

1. Write down situations where you made mistakes during a game or practice and reflect on what went wrong and why.

_____

_____

_____

_____

_____

_____

_____

_____

_____

2. Come up with alternative strategies or solutions you could have implemented to avoid or rectify those mistakes.

_____

_____

_____

_____

_____

_____

_____

_____

_____

_____

_____

_____

_____

⚽ Activity: Grit Building Exercise

1. Set a long-term goal for your soccer skills. For example, "I want to become an expert at _____."

_____

_____

_____

_____

_____

_____

_____

_____

_____

2. Break down your goal into smaller, achievable targets. For example, "I will practice _____ every day for _____ minutes."

_____

_____

_____

_____

_____

_____

_____

_____

_____

3. Celebrate each milestone you reach. For example, when you achieve one of your targets, _____ and _____ it in detail.

_____

_____

_____

_____

_____

_____

4. When facing challenges, remind yourself of how much you _____ playing soccer and _____ after a great match.

Chapter 3
The Power of Visualization

How Athletes Use Visualization

Have you ever heard of the phrase, "If you can see it, you can be it"? This is the magic of visualization. Visualization is the ability to create a vivid picture in your mind of whatever you want to happen or achieve. It's like creating a preview of your life's upcoming moments. It's a superpower that you can use to guide your actions and decisions.

Did you know that many of the world's top athletes use visualization to enhance their performance? For example, in soccer, players imagine scoring amazing goals or making incredible saves. They close their eyes and picture themselves shooting the perfect shot. They imagine the ball going right through the back of the net, just like they want it to. It helps them feel more confident and prepared when they're actually in the game.

Athletes with a growth mindset - as we mentioned in the first chapters, those who believe that they can improve with effort and practice - often use visualization as a tool to help them reach their goals. They picture themselves achieving their goals, and that mental image helps drive them towards success.

Visualization can also be used by athletes to run challenging scenarios in their mind, and prepare themselves for worst case scenarios. This helps them to be ready to tackle those challenges head-on when they arise.
Think of it this way: visualization is like a rehearsal. By visualizing, athletes are practicing in their minds, so when the real game comes, they've already performed it in their head, making the actual performance feel more familiar and less daunting.

Visualization as an Exercise: Scoring the Perfect Goal

Now, let's try visualization as an exercise. Close your eyes and imagine you're playing your favorite sport. For this example, let's say it's soccer.

Picture yourself on the field. Feel the weight of your cleats on the grass, hear the roar of the crowd, and smell the fresh air. Now, see the soccer ball at your feet.

You're about to take the most important shot of the game. Visualize yourself dribbling the ball towards the goal, your heart pounding in your chest. You see the goalkeeper trying to anticipate your move, but you're focused, ready.

Now, you take the shot. Visualize the ball sailing through the air, past the goalkeeper, and into the net. Hear the crowd roar as you score the perfect goal. Feel the joy and satisfaction of achieving what you visualized.

Now, open your eyes. You've just scored the perfect goal, in your mind. The more you practice this visualization, the more likely you are to score that goal in real life.

Remember, visualization is not just about sports. You can use it for any aspect of your life, whether it's acing a test, nailing a presentation, or making new friends. The power of visualization is in your hands. So, close your eyes, picture your success, and then go out and make it happen!

Using Visualization as part of your pre-game routine

Warming up your muscles is an essential part of a soccer pre-game routine. However, it's equally crucial to "warm up" your mind, by visualizing your goals for the game: dribbling past opponents, making goals, etc. Take a moment before each training session or game to close your eyes and visualize yourself executing skills flawlessly, scoring goals, and making crucial plays. As you vividly imagine these scenarios, your mind starts to believe that they are possible. This mental rehearsal strengthens the neural pathways in your brain, enhancing muscle memory and boosting your overall performance. So, dream big, set realistic goals, and visualize yourself achieving them with every ounce of determination you possess.

⚽ Activity: Visualize your favorite moment playing soccer

1. Write down one of your favorite moments playing soccer. Describe in detail the day (was it sunny? Was it in the

morning or afternoon?); how were you feeling before the game (were you nervous? excited?); how were you feeling during and after the game? Write as much as you remember about what happened that made it your favorite moment.

⚽ Activity: Create a pre-game routine visualization exercise

1. Start by recalling the time you made your favorite goal, assist, or save. Try to remember that moment in as much detail as you can. Write down how it felt before and after. Try to remember it as it was on video, and you are watching it to analyze each moment, each movement, and also all the emotions that you felt after it. Write it down, and start using this exercise as part of your pre-game routine.

Chapter 4
Relaxation and Focus

The Importance of Relaxation for Performance

We are going to talk about an often overlooked but essential aspect of your game - **relaxation**.

You might be wondering, "Relaxation? But isn't soccer all about being active and energetic?" Absolutely, soccer is definitely about action, but relaxation plays a critical role in your performance too.

Imagine you're a top-class striker, always ready to score the next goal. You've got the ball, the goalpost is in sight, and you're sprinting towards it. But your energy is draining, your focus is wavering, and suddenly, you miss the shot. Why? Because you didn't give yourself a chance to rest, to recharge, to relax.

So when would you be able to relax during the game? I would say any moment that you have time to catch your breath, and consciously think you are using those moments to relax. Or during that brief pause you get when the referee blows the whistle. The game stops, you catch your breath, your muscles relax, and then you're ready to get back into action, refreshed and focused. It is important to use those moments of pause, to avoid getting mentally and physically exhausted.

So, remember to take those small breaks, and during your day to day as well. Enjoy a quiet moment, listen to some calming music, or simply close your eyes and let your mind wander. These relaxation moments can be your secret weapon to staying centered, and at the top of your game.

Breathing Techniques for Stress Reduction

Now, let's move on to another great tool for relaxation - breathing techniques. Breathing is the number one body regulator; the way you breathe can significantly impact how you feel, physically and mentally.

One technique that's particularly useful for focus and relaxation is called "Square Breathing." Here's how it works:

1. Sit in a comfortable position.
2. Close your eyes and take a deep breath, counting to 4 in your head as you inhale.
3. Hold your breath for another count of 4.
4. Slowly exhale to a count of 4.
5. Pause for a count of 4 before taking another breath.
6. Repeat this cycle a few times.

Why is it called Square Breathing? Because just like a square has four equal sides, this technique has four steps, each done for a count of four.

This technique can work wonders when you're feeling anxious before a big game, or when you're trying to refocus during halftime. It slows down your heart rate and sends a message to your brain, saying, "It's cool-down time!"

Remember, relaxation and focus are as crucial as your dribbling and shooting skills. By incorporating relaxation moments and practicing square breathing, you'll not only be leveling up your performance but also enjoying the game more. So, relax, breathe, and take pleasure in every moment on and off the field.

Mindfulness for Boosting Focus

Now, let's talk about something called mindfulness. **Mindfulness** is all about paying attention to what's happening right now, at this moment, without any judgment. It's about being fully present and aware.

"But how can this help me in soccer?" you may ask. Great question! In soccer, it's essential to be fully focused on the game as it unfolds. You have to be aware of the ball, your teammates, your opponents, and the goal.

Sometimes, when something goes wrong—like when the opposing team scores a goal, the referee makes an "unfair" call, or you lose the ball to an opponent—it's easy to lose focus and dwell on what went wrong. This "distraction" doesn't benefit you in the moment because your mind is fixated on the negative rather than being present and prepared for action and what comes next.

Practicing mindfulness will help you make better and more accurate choices, as your mind is fully focused and aware, allowing you to be 100% engaged in the game at all times.

Here's a simple mindfulness exercise you can do:

1. Find a quiet spot and sit comfortably.
2. Close your eyes and take a few deep breaths.
3. Try to focus on the sensation of the breath coming in and going out. Feel the rise and fall of your chest or the sensation of the air passing through your nostrils.
4. Your mind will wander—that's totally normal. When it does, gently bring your attention back to your breath, without any judgment.
5. Practice this for a few minutes each day.

Now, let's apply this to soccer. When you're on the field, take a moment to become fully aware of the present. Feel the grass under your feet, listen to the sounds around you—the cheers, the whistle, the thump of the ball. Feel the weight of the ball against your foot. By doing this, you're practicing mindfulness.

Mindfulness practice can help you keep your focus on the game, reducing distractions and improving your performance. Just as hitting the gym makes your muscles stronger, training your brain with mindfulness exercises makes it sharper and more focused.

Imagine your brain as a muscle that needs regular workouts to stay in top shape. At the beginning, when you start practicing mindfulness, your mind might wander all over the place, just like when you first lift weights and struggle to lift heavier ones. But as you keep at it, your brain gets stronger and more disciplined.

Eventually, staying focused becomes easier, and distractions have less power over you. And the best part? Being mindful of the moment not only boosts your performance on the field but also makes playing the game even more enjoyable. You'll feel completely absorbed in the action, fully immersed in every pass, kick, and goal.

So there you have it! Relaxation, breathing techniques, and mindfulness—three powerful tools to boost your performance and enjoyment of the beautiful game. Remember, soccer is not just about physical strength and tactics; it's also about mental well-being and focus. So, relax, breathe, stay mindful, and most importantly, have fun out there on the field!

ACTIVITY: MINDFUL BREATHING

1. Find a quiet and comfortable space.
2. Write down how you are feeling. Rate it from 1 to 10 (1= feeling anxious or angry 10= feeling calm and happy)
2. Sit or lie down in a relaxed position.
3. Close your eyes and take a deep breath in through your nose, counting to four.
4. Hold your breath for a count of four.
5. Slowly exhale through your mouth, counting to four.
6. Repeat this breathing pattern for several minutes, focusing your attention solely on your breath.
7. Afterward, reflect and write a paragraph about how you felt during the practice. Did you notice any changes in your body or mind? How did it affect your focus and relaxation?
8. Rate from 1 to 10 how you are feeling after the exercise (1= feeling anxious or angry 10= feeling calm and happy). Did the number change from the start of the exercise? Are you feeling differently? It is ok if you didn't notice a change; becoming more aware or attuned to your feelings is the ultimate goal.

⚽ ACTIVITY: VISUALIZATION OF A POSITIVE PAST PERFORMANCE

1. Find a quiet and comfortable space.
2. Close your eyes and take a few deep breaths to calm your mind.
3. Imagine yourself on the soccer field, fully immersed in a game.
4. Visualize executing various soccer skills with precision, such as passing, shooting, and dribbling.
5. Picture yourself feeling confident, focused, and relaxed during the game.
6. Engage all your senses - visualize the sights, sounds, and even the smell of the soccer field.
7. Afterward, reflect and write a paragraph about your visualization experience. Did it enhance your focus and relaxation? How did it make you feel about your soccer abilities?

⚽ Activity: Progressive Muscle Relaxation

1. Find a quiet and comfortable space.
2. Sit or lie down in a relaxed position.
3. Close your eyes and take a few deep breaths.
4. Starting from your toes, tense the muscles in your feet for a few seconds, then release the tension while exhaling.
5. Slowly work your way up through each muscle group, tensing and releasing one at a time, including your legs, abdomen, arms, and face.
6. Pay attention to the sensation of relaxation as you release the tension from each muscle group.
7. Afterward, reflect and write a paragraph about how your body and mind felt during the practice. Did you experience a heightened sense of relaxation and focus? How might this technique benefit your soccer performance?

Chapter 5
Reframing Negative Thoughts

The Power of Positive Thinking

In this chapter we will work on one of the main skills needed in soccer, and that has nothing to do with your physical ability. This skill is equally as important but often overlooked and underestimated - the power of positive thinking.

Positive thinking is like a coach inside your head, cheering you on, reminding you that every pass, every goal, every victory, and even every loss, is a chance to learn and grow. It's about seeing the field not just as a place where a game is won or lost, but as a platform where you can develop your skills, foster teamwork, and build resilience. It's understanding that even when it rains, you're not just getting wet; you're learning to play in challenging conditions. And it's knowing that every time you miss a goal, you're not failing but discovering ways to improve your skills.

Positive thinking doesn't mean ignoring the hard parts, but rather embracing them as opportunities. Remember, a positive mindset can turn hurdles into stepping stones, fostering a passion for self-improvement, persistence, and a love for the game that extends beyond the soccer field.

From Negative to Positive: Soccer Scenarios Exercises

You might be wondering how we can work on what your mind is thinking. The first step is to recognize when a negative thought popped into your mind. Once you realize that, you can switch that thought to a more positive one. Let's put this into practice with some soccer scenarios as examples.

Scenario 1:
Imagine you're in a match. You've been playing well, but you miss an important goal. Negative thoughts start creeping in, "I'm terrible at this. I let my team down."

Now, let's reframe this. Instead of beating yourself up, think, "I missed that goal, but I've scored before, and I will again. **This is not a failure, but a chance to be mentally stronger and improve.**"

Scenario 2:
Your team is behind, and it's almost the end of the game. You start thinking, "We're going to lose. There's no point in trying anymore."

Time for some positive reframe! Instead, tell yourself, "There's still time on the clock. Every moment in the game is an opportunity. Let's give it our best shot! **Even if we don't win, the practice of playing will make us better**"

Scenario 3:
You've been benched for a crucial game. You can't help but think, "I'm not good enough. That's why I'm not playing."

Let's swap that with a positive mindset. Consider this, "**This is an opportunity to observe and learn. I'll use this time to understand the game better and come back stronger.**"

Remember, soccer is not just about the physical game. It's also a mental game. The way you think can strongly affect the way you play. Remember that focusing on your mind will give you an additional skill to perform even better.

Keep playing, keep thinking positively, and remember - every game, every moment is an opportunity to learn, grow, and shine. You've got this!

⚽ ACTIVITY: RECOGNIZING POSITIVE ACTIONS

1. Think back to your last soccer game.
2. Try to remember positive actions that happened, such as good sportsmanship, fair play, teamwork, and positive communication.
3. Write down or make a list of the positive actions you observed.
4. Reflect on why these actions were positive and how they impacted the game. Write a paragraph describing them and the positive impact they had during the game.

Example:
One player from the other team helped one of our players who fell down by offering a hand to help him get back up. This act of being a good sport showed respect for us, the opponent, and created a good atmosphere on the field. Also, I noticed our players were giving high-fives after

scoring a goal, showing our great teamwork and friendship. These positive actions showed respect among all, making us enjoy the game more.

⚽ ACTIVITY: TRANSFORMING NEGATIVE SCENARIOS

1. Imagine a negative scenario that could happen during a soccer match, such as a teammate making a mistake or an opponent playing rough.
2. Write down the negative scenario in detail, describing the actions and the emotions associated with it.
3. Think on how this negative scenario could be transformed into a positive outcome.
4. Write a paragraph explaining how you would approach and handle the negative scenario to achieve a positive outcome.

Example:
A negative scenario that could happen during a soccer match is when a teammate makes a mistake that leads to the opposing team scoring a goal. In this situation, it's key to transform the negativity into a positive outcome. Instead of blaming or criticizing the teammate, I would remind them that mistakes happen to everyone and that we can still work on turning things around. By offering support and reassurance, we can work together as a team to overcome that setback and regain our confidence. This positive approach would help our team to keep trying to bounce

back together, stronger and more determined to change things around.

In the case of an opponent playing rough, I would tell my teammates to stay focused and calm. If we were to engage in fouling, our game would suffer, and we would not be able to perform at our best. By keeping our head in the game, and not retaliating, we would be able to put our energy in playing for the win.

Chapter 6
The Power of Purpose

Finding Purpose

In this chapter, we're going to talk about something that might not seem immediately related to soccer but trust me, it's a game-changer. We're going to talk about "**Purpose**".

Purpose is like the North Star. It guides us, it gives us direction, and it helps us navigate through the toughest storms. In soccer, having a purpose means knowing **why you play the game, what drives you, and what you hope to achieve**.

Let's think about it this way. Imagine you're in the middle of an intense match. The score is tied, and there's just a few minutes left on the clock. You're tired, your legs are burning, and you can barely catch your breath. In this moment, it's your purpose that will keep you going. It's your purpose that will give you that extra burst of energy you need to sprint towards the goal, to make that crucial tackle, or to take that game-winning shot.

But how do you find your purpose? Well, it's a journey, not a destination. It's about asking yourself some important questions. Why do you love soccer? What brings you joy when you're on the pitch? Is it the thrill of the game, the camaraderie with your teammates, the roar of the crowd, or the satisfaction of seeing your hard work pay off?

Your purpose is deeply personal, and it's something only you can discover. It might take some time, and your purpose might even evolve as you grow and change. That's okay! The important thing is to keep asking, keep exploring, and keep pushing yourself to be the best player – and person – you can be.

Remember, becoming a stronger soccer player isn't just about physical strength. It's about mental and emotional strength, too. It's about resilience, determination, and grit. And having a purpose can fuel all of these qualities.

So, aim high! Play with purpose, train with purpose, and live with purpose. Whether on the soccer field or off it, strive to make every moment count.

⚽ ACTIVITY: THE "WHY?" GAME

1. Here's a fun activity to kick things off. Ask yourself, "Why do I play soccer?" Write down your immediate answer below.

_____

_____

_____

_____

_____

_____

_____

_____

_____

Now, ask "Why?" to your answer. Keep asking "Why?" to each new answer until you've asked it 5 times in total. This will help you dig deeper into your motivations.

1. Why?

_____

_____

_____

_____

_____

_____

_____

2. Why?

_____

_____

_____

3. Why?

4. Why?

5. Why?

⚽ Activity: My Soccer Mantra

A mantra is a phrase that can inspire and motivate you. Create a soccer mantra that aligns with your purpose. This should be something you can repeat to yourself during training or a match, especially when things get tough.

Write your soccer mantra here:

_____

_____

_____

Now, write a short paragraph on why you have chosen this mantra and how it connects to your purpose.

_____

_____

_____

_____

_____

_____

_____

_____

_____

⚽ Activity: The Purpose Pyramid

In this activity, we're going to build a purpose pyramid. In each section, fill in the blanks with your answers.

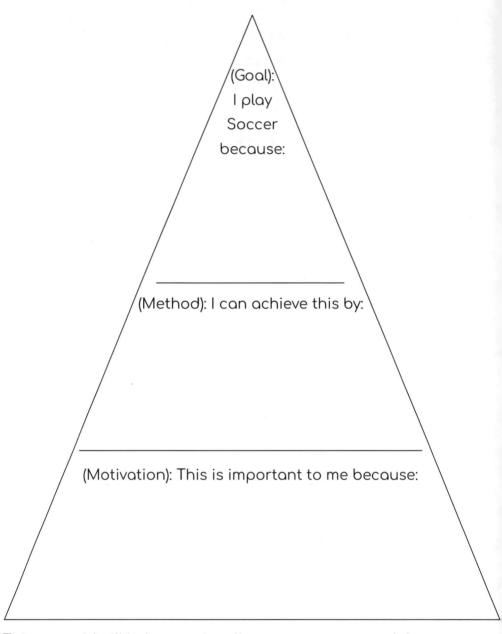

This pyramid will help you visualize your purpose and the steps you need to take to reach your goal.

⚽ ACTIVITY: THE SOCCER STAR STORY

Imagine you're a famous soccer player being interviewed after a big game. In the interview, you're asked about your purpose in playing soccer.

Fill in the blanks to complete your interview:

Reporter: "What drives you to play soccer?"

You: "What drives me is

_____

_____

_____

_____

_____

_____

Reporter: "How does that help you in challenging situations?"

You: "When faced with challenges, I

Chapter 7
Passion & Fight: Giving Everything On The Pitch

Leave It All On The Field

You've probably heard the phrase "leave it all on the field" before. It's a common saying in sports, but especially in soccer. But what does it actually mean? To me, it means playing with passion and fighting with all you've got. It means giving your absolute best every time you step on the field, and never holding back. It's about being determined to win, but also being prepared to lose. It's about learning to endure, to strive, and to grow, regardless of the outcome.

Passion is the fuel that drives us to do what we do. It's the love for the game that gets us to hard training sessions and keeps us going when our legs feel like they're about to give in. It's the thrill of scoring a goal, the satisfaction of making a great pass, and the joy of being part of a team. Passion is what keeps us coming back to the pitch, day after day, week after week.

But passion alone isn't enough. You also need to have the fight in you. You need to be willing to push yourself to your limits, to battle for every ball, to stand up to your opponents, and to never give up, no matter how tough things get.

Now, when I talk about fighting, I don't mean getting into physical fights with your opponents. No, the fight I'm talking about is an internal one. It's the battle between your mind and your body, between what you think you can do and what you can actually do. It's about pushing through the pain, the fatigue, and the doubt, and coming out stronger on the other side.

Let me share a personal story with you. I remember a particular match my son played. They were coming from a losing streak, and were two goals up, but then the opposing team tied. You could see that most of the players were already thinking "that's it - we are going to lose this game too", and their performance wasn't as strong as at the start.

My son, at that time, was being subbed, and I could see his frustration for being on the sidelines, and wanting badly to help his team win. When he finally was put back in the game, you could see that fire fueling him. In the end, he got a chance and did not doubt himself to take it: he scored the most amazing goal he's ever made, a powerful strike outside the box that crossed to the top corner of the net, and gave his team the win. That day, he exemplified the power of passion and fight.

Of course, there will be matches where you won't win, where no matter how hard you fight, the opposing team might simply be better. But the key is to learn that losing isn't the end of the world. In fact, it's an opportunity to learn, to grow, to become stronger. Every time you lose, you learn something new about yourself, about your team, and about the game. You learn what you need to improve, and you get a chance to come back stronger.

So, how can you cultivate passion and fight? Start by finding what you love about soccer. Is it the thrill of scoring a goal? The camaraderie of being part of a team? The challenge of improving your skills? Whatever it is, hold onto that love, and let it fuel your passion.

As for the fight, it's all about attitude. Believe in yourself, push yourself to your limits, and never give up. When things get tough, remember why you love the game, and let that love drive you to keep going.

Has it ever happened that you were put on the bench as a sub? How did you feel about it? This is a great opportunity to explore your attitude and mindset. Thinking of yourself as someone that can get in the game and make a difference -being a true game changer- can be crucial to the game.

Remember, soccer is more than just a game. It's a journey, a journey of passion, fight, and personal growth. So, play with all your heart, give everything you've got in practices and on the pitch, and I promise, you'll come out a stronger player, and a stronger person.

And finally, always remember this: Win or lose, it's the passion and fight you put into the game that truly defines you as a player. So, go out there, play with all your heart, and leave it all on the pitch.

⚽ Activity: Igniting your Passion and Fight

Take some time to reflect on your own passion for soccer and the level of fight you bring to each match. Answer the following questions in a paragraph:

1. What is it about soccer that you are most passionate about? Is it the thrill of scoring goals, the teamwork, the competition, or something else? Explain why this aspect of the game ignites your passion.

_____

_____

_____

_____

_____

_____

_____

_____

_____

_____

_____

_____

_____

_____

_____

_____

_____

_____

2. How do you currently demonstrate fight on the pitch? Do you push yourself to your limits, never give up, and always give your best effort? Provide specific examples from your recent matches or training sessions.

_____

_____

_____

_____

_____

3. What are some areas where you can improve your passion and fight in soccer? Are there any situations or moments in games where you tend to lose focus or motivation? Identify these areas and think about how you can overcome them.

_____

_____

_____

_____

_____

_____

Chapter 8
Teamwork

The Essence of Teamwork

As a soccer player, you're part of something bigger than yourself—a team. Teamwork is the secret ingredient that can turn a group of individuals, with different skills, into an unstoppable force. It's about combining your unique abilities with those of your teammates, understanding their strengths, and supporting one another on and off the field.

Together, you can achieve great things that would be impossible on your own. By focusing on teamwork, you'll unlock a whole new level of soccer. You'll learn to trust your teammates, communicate effectively, and embrace each other's strengths. Together, you'll create a powerhouse of skills and strategies that will make you unstoppable.

Trust and Communication

Trust is the bedrock of any successful team. Just like a well-oiled machine, every part needs to work in harmony and together. Trusting your teammates means knowing that they have your back and believing in their abilities.

Communication is the key that unlocks this trust. Whether it's shouting out cheers, praise, or instructions during a game, or having open, honest conversations during practice, effective communication strengthens the bonds within your team.

It is also important to have a check-in during halftime. It is an opportunity for encouragement, to highlight what has been working or what can be improved, always approaching it from a positive perspective. This chat is important to increase the team's connection, and it will reinforce working together towards a unified goal: having a great game together.

Embracing Roles and Responsibilities

A team is made up of players with diverse skills and talents. Each member has a unique role and responsibility that contributes to the bigger picture.

Embrace your role and strive to excel in it. Whether you're a striker, a midfielder, a defender, or a goalkeeper, understand how your role fits into the team's strategy, and give it everything you've got. By doing so, you'll create a seamless connection between your teammates, and maximize your collective potential.

Unity in Diversity

Every player on your team brings something special to the table. Different playing styles, backgrounds, and perspectives can provide fresh ideas, innovative strategies, and a wider range of skills.

Recognize the diversity within your team and celebrate it. This will create a supportive environment where everyone feels valued and motivated to give their best, for the good of the team.

Supporting Each Other

Soccer is a game of ups and downs. There will be moments of triumph and moments of disappointment. During tough times, supporting your teammates becomes even more crucial. Lift each other up, offer words of encouragement, offer a shoulder to lean on during defeats, and also be there to celebrate victories. Remember, a strong team is built on the foundation of unwavering support and camaraderie.

Celebrating Success

In soccer, victories are meant to be shared and celebrated. When your team accomplishes a goal, take a moment to enjoy and acknowledge the hard work that got you there. Celebrations not only boost team morale but also create lasting memories and bonds that will strengthen your unity in future games.

Resilience in the Face of Challenges

Teamwork isn't just about winning games; it's about learning from setbacks and bouncing back stronger, together.

Soccer, like life, is full of challenges. It's during those challenging moments that your team's true strength shines through. Embrace adversity as an opportunity to learn, grow, and come back with renewed determination. Remember, a team that faces challenges together is a team that can conquer anything.

Teamwork is an ongoing process, and it requires continuous effort and dedication from every player. Reflect on your strengths, communication skills, and supportiveness, and think about the same traits of your teammates. By actively working on these areas, you'll become an invaluable member of your team and contribute to its success.

⚽ Activity: Becoming a Better Team Player

1- Understanding Your Role

In this activity, you will reflect on your role within the team and gain a deeper understanding of how you can contribute effectively. Fill in the blanks with your own answers.

1. My primary position on the team is

_____

_____

_____

2. Three key skills or strengths I bring to the team are

_____

_____

_____

_____

_____

_____

3. One area I would like to improve upon is

_____

_____

_____

_____

_____

_____

4. How can I utilize my strengths to benefit the team?

_____

_____

_____

_____

_____

_____

5. How can I work on improving the area I identified in question 3?

_____

_____

_____

_____

_____

_____

6. List three specific actions you can take to enhance your role on the team:

_____

_____

_____

_____

_____

_____

_____

_____

_____

_____

2 - Effective Communication

Communication is a vital aspect of teamwork. In this activity, think about how you can improve your communication skills within the team. Fill in the blanks to complete the sentences.

1. During a game, I can effectively communicate with my teammates by

_____

_____

_____

_____

_____

2. In practice, I can contribute to better communication by

_____

_____

_____

_____

_____

_____

_____

_____

_____

3. One challenge I face when it comes to communication is

_____

_____

_____

_____

_____

To overcome this challenge, I can

_____

_____

_____

_____

_____

3 - Supporting Your Teammates

Being a supportive teammate is crucial for a strong team dynamic. Complete the sentences by filling in the blanks with your own ideas.

1. One way I can support my teammates during a game is

_____

_____

_____

_____

_____

2. Off the field, I can show support by

_____

_____

_____

_____

_____

3. When a teammate makes a mistake, I can offer
encouragement by

_____

_____

_____

_____

4. Name three ways you can demonstrate empathy and understanding towards your teammates:

_____

_____

_____

_____

_____

_____

_____

_____

_____

_____

_____

_____

Chapter 9
Be a Leader In Your Team

Being a Leader

There's one more thing that can make you stand out even more on the soccer field - **being a leader**. It's not about being the loudest or the bossiest, but about **guiding your team, making smart decisions, and setting an example with your actions**.

So, how do you become a leader in your team? We talked in the previous chapter about learning the different skills your teammates have. Knowing each of them and what they bring to the table, is important for becoming a great team leader.

Here are some practical steps to get you started:

Step 1: Understand Your Teammates

Every effective leader knows the strengths and weaknesses of their team. Spend time with your teammates off the field. Get to know them. Understand their skills, their hopes, and their fears. This understanding can help you guide them better on the field. Remember, a team is like a jigsaw puzzle. Each piece is unique and essential for completing the picture.

Step 2: Show Respect

Treat everyone with respect, whether they're the best player on the team or the one who's still learning. Nobody likes a show-off or a bully. You can earn respect by showing it. This way, when you speak or act, your teammates will pay attention.

Step 3: Be a Role Model

As a leader, you need to lead by example. That means being the first one to arrive at practice and the last one to leave. It means working hard, staying positive, and never giving up, even when things get tough. It's not about being perfect; it's about showing that you're committed to giving your best and improving.

Step 4: Communicate Effectively

As we mentioned before, communication is key in soccer. Let your teammates know when they're doing well, and offer constructive feedback when they need it. Use clear and simple language. Remember, it's not what you say, but how you say it that matters.

Step 5: Be Optimistic Yet Realistic

Stay positive, but also be realistic. If you're losing a game, don't pretend everything's great. Acknowledge the situation, but remind your team that you can still turn things around, or use what is happening to practice and become more resilient. Mistakes and losses are opportunities to learn and improve.

Step 6: Make Decisions for the Team

Sometimes, you'll need to make tough decisions for the good of the team. It might mean taking a penalty kick instead of your best friend, or defending instead of attacking. These decisions may not be popular, but they're necessary. As a leader, your goal is to do what's best for the team, not just for yourself.

Step 7: Encourage and Acknowledge Your Team Members

As a leader, it's crucial to boost your team's morale and acknowledge their efforts. Encouragement goes a long way in making your teammates feel valued and motivated. When they make a good move, score a goal, or even just show improvement, make sure to let them know you noticed. A simple "great job" or "well done" can significantly lift their spirits.

But don't stop at praising good outcomes. Remember to acknowledge effort too. Even when a teammate misses a goal or makes a mistake, if they tried their best, that effort deserves recognition. This will teach your teammates that it's okay to make mistakes and that effort is just as important as the result.

Acknowledging your team members also means celebrating their individual strengths. Everyone has something unique to bring to the team, whether it's speed, agility, strategic thinking, or a positive attitude. Recognizing these strengths helps to build a stronger, more cohesive team.

And don't forget, encouragement should also extend to times off the field. Stand by your team members when they're facing personal challenges. Show them that you're not just a team on the field, but also a team in life.

Incorporating this step will make you a more empathetic and supportive leader, fostering a more positive and motivated team environment. Remember, **a leader is as strong as the team, and a team is as strong as its leader.**

Becoming a leader is a journey. It won't happen overnight, but with time, patience, and practice, you can become the kind of leader your team needs. And remember, being a leader isn't about being the star; it's about helping your team shine.

⚽ ACTIVITY: TEAMMATE APPRECIATION EXERCISE

Reflect on your last soccer practice or game. Think about each of your teammates and identify one thing they did well or one strength they showcased. It could be a great pass, a strong defense, or even their constant encouragement. Write a paragraph about each teammate and what you appreciated about their performance. If you choose to share these appreciations with your teammates, this could also encourage a culture of appreciation within your team

_____

_____

_____

_____

_____

_____

_____

_____

Activity 2: Communication Challenge

In your next practice, set a personal goal to improve your communication. It could be cheering for your teammates, giving constructive feedback, or guiding your team with clear instructions during the game.

After the practice, write a paragraph about how you felt while doing this. Was it easy or hard for you? How did your teammates respond? Did it make a difference to the game? Reflecting on these questions will help you understand the power of effective communication and identify areas where you can improve.

Chapter 10
Unleashing Your True Potential

Building Confidence

Have you ever watched your favorite players glide across the field, scoring goals with what seems like effortless precision? They play with a certain magic, a sparkle that goes beyond their skills. That, my friends, is the glow of confidence.

Confidence is your silent partner in soccer, the one that runs alongside you, whispering, "You've got this!" every time you touch the ball. It's not just about believing you can play well; it's about knowing it deep in your bones.

But let's get real for a second. Confidence doesn't just show up one day, wearing a cape, ready to save the day. It's also like a muscle, and needs to be built up, trained, and flexed. So, how do we start?

First, let's debunk a myth: Confidence is not something you're born with—it's something you create. And the building blocks? They're your experiences, your practice, and your mindset.

Imagine you're standing on the field, the green grass beneath your feet, the cheers of the crowd in your ears. Maybe your palms are sweaty, and that's okay—because guess what? Even the pros get nervous. The key is to use that energy to your advantage. Turn it into excitement, into power. That's the first secret of confidence: It's okay to be nervous. Nervous means you care. And when you care, you play with passion.

To believe in yourself, start by setting realistic goals. Not just the grand dreams of scoring the winning goal in a championship but daily, achievable goals that lead you there. Each time you tick a goal off your list, you're building a ladder to success, step by step. Celebrate every small victory, every mastered skill, and every lesson learned from a less-than-perfect play. These are all milestones of your journey.

Confidence is also about preparation. The more you practice, the more you learn about the ball's behavior, the more you understand the game's flow, the more confident you'll become. Practice isn't just repetition; it's an act of faith in your future self. When you practice, you're telling yourself, "I believe in my ability to improve."

Practice is also about setting challenges for yourself, pushing your limits, and then pushing them a little more. When you master a new move or finally nail that shot you've been working on for weeks, it's like adding a supercharger to your confidence engine.

But what about those days when nothing goes right? When the ball seems to have a mind of its own, and your feet can't seem to keep up? That is where your champion mindset comes in. Take a breath, shake it off, and remind yourself that one bad day doesn't define you. Champions aren't made from a single game; they're made from a season of games, a career of games.

And guess what? Mistakes are part of the journey. Each one is a mini-lesson wrapped up in a "Try Again" opportunity. Remember, every soccer star was once a beginner, stumbling over the ball, missing shots, but they didn't let that stop them. They used it as fuel to grow stronger, and so will you.

As you can see, building confidence isn't about never falling; it's about knowing that when you do, you have the courage to stand back up, dust off your knees, and say, "Bring it on!"

All soccer legends got there with hours of practice, dedication, and the willingness to learn from every mistake. So remember that each time you practice, or you are facing challenges, you're not just working on your dribbling or your free kicks, you're also building your mental toughness and confidence, which is key to your performance.

Confidence begins in your mind, and one powerful tactic to harness it is through visualization. Imagine the roar of the crowd as you zig zag past defenders, the satisfying thud of the ball hitting the back of the net from your impeccable shot, or the thrill of stopping a goal with a flawless save. By visualizing these moments of triumph, you're not just daydreaming; you're constructing neural bridges to success. This mental rehearsal instills a deep-seated confidence, as your brain sets the envisioned achievements as preparatory blueprints. When the moment of action arrives, your mind is ready, conditioned for success by the confidence you've cultivated through the vivid imagery of your victories.

HAVING FUN

Fun while playing soccer is not just allowed; it's mandatory! Soccer is a game, and games are meant to be enjoyed. When the whistle blows and the game starts, let that joy infuse every step you take on the field.

Keep the fun alive by mixing things up. Try new moves, play different positions, or even switch up your routine with a game of soccer tennis or a friendly shootout. By keeping things fresh, you're not only becoming a more versatile player, you're also reminding yourself why you fell in love with soccer in the first place.

Fun is infectious, and, after all, soccer is a team sport. Share your joy with teammates, celebrate their successes as if they were your own, and lift each other up when the going gets tough. A team that has fun together forms bonds stronger than any defensive line.

But let's be real—sometimes, soccer can be frustrating. Missed opportunities, tough losses, and off days can cast a shadow over the joy of the game. When this happens, step back and find perspective. Reflect on what soccer truly means to you, beyond the wins and losses. Find the silver linings and lessons within every challenge.

And remember, having fun doesn't mean taking it easy. Channel your joy into passion and your passion into determination. Play each game as if it's your last, but play with the lightness of heart as if it's always your first. That balance between dedication and delight is where the true magic happens.

Pulling it all Together

It is time to reflect on the lessons we've learned and the skills we've sharpened. Soccer isn't just a game of scoring goals and making saves. It's a showcase of resilience, determination, and the relentless pursuit of growth.

We began our journey learning that growth is not always about winning or losing. It's about developing skills, adapting, and growing stronger with every challenge. Just as a ball needs a good kick to soar into the sky, we too need a push to break free from our comfort zones. Remember, every great soccer player was once a beginner who refused to give up, and who put a lot of effort and work into becoming successful.

We also learned about grit, which acts as your invisible armor. It protects you from failure, disappointment, and negativity. It's not something you're born with, but something you build with effort and perseverance. It allows you to keep pushing, and keep fighting, even when the odds are all against you.

Then we explored 'The Power of Visualization.' Visualization is not magic, but a powerful tool that can transform your performance. If you can imagine yourself scoring that perfect goal or making that impossible save, it is much more likely to happen in real life. Seeing it in your mind, is the first step to make it happen on the field.

'Relaxation and Focus' taught us that soccer isn't just about physical strength. It's a mental game too. Your mind is like a captain steering the ship of your body. If it's calm and focused, it can guide you through the trickiest situations on the field. So breathe, relax, and let your mind take the lead.

Next, we were introduced to 'Reframing Negative Thoughts.' Remember when you missed a goal or made a wrong pass? It felt bad, didn't it? But we learned that it's okay to make mistakes. Instead of letting them pull you down, use them as stepping stones to climb higher. Every mistake is a lesson in disguise.

We also discussed 'Purpose in Soccer.' Soccer is more than a game. It's a passion, a dream, a life lesson. It teaches you about winning and losing, about hard work and patience, about failure and success. When you play, play with a purpose. Play because you love the game, because you want to grow, and because you want to be the best version of yourself.

When it came to understanding what drives us to become a great soccer player, we learned that passion is the fire that fuels your performance on the soccer field. And fight is never giving up, no matter how bad things look. There are always lessons to learn, practices to improve, and goals to work towards. Remember that passion and fight can also inspire your teammates and elevate the level of play for everyone.

In 'Teamwork,' we discovered the power of unity. Soccer is a team sport, and every player is a vital piece of the puzzle. Without each other, we are incomplete - we need each other! When you play, play for your team, because a team that plays together, stays together, and wins together.

We also discovered the importance of being a leader, and how it can positively impact your whole team. A leader plays a crucial role in guiding, motivating, and inspiring the team towards a common goal. By using key leadership qualities like effective communication, empathy, decision-making skills, and the ability to lead by example, a leader can create a great environment for growth and collaboration within the team. Ultimately, a strong leader has the power to elevate the performance and morale of the entire team, leading to it playing in sync, connecting passes, and having more chances to score.

As you turn the pages of this book and step onto the field to write your own story, carry these final thoughts with you: **believe in yourself, even when it feels like no one else does.** Have fun, even when the pressure mounts. These aren't just tips for becoming a stronger soccer player; they are life lessons that will guide you through the victories and defeats, the cheers and the silence, the sunlit days and the stormy nights.

Finally, let's talk about the power of positivity. Your thoughts have the power to lift you up or bring you down. Choose to focus on what you can do, not what you can't. Set your sights on your goals, and let them pull you forward. When you believe in yourself, really believe, that's when the magic happens. That's when you become unstoppable.

So, lace up your cleats, pull on your jersey, and step onto that field with your head held high. You're not just playing soccer; you're building the unshakeable confidence of a champion. And remember, I believe in you, your coaches believe in you, your teammates believe in you, and it's time for you to believe in you too.

Because in the heart-pounding, goal-scoring, grass-stained glory of soccer, confidence is the game-changer—and you've got what it takes to be a game-changer, too.

The journey has been incredible, hasn't it? Remember, in soccer, as in life, it's not about where you start, but where you finish. So keep learning, keep growing, and keep playing.

You are unstoppable.

Now go out there, and unleash your true potential!

WORKBOOK

Creating a pre-game routine is essential, as it helps you physically and mentally prepare for the game. A good routine can improve focus, reduce anxiety, and enhance performance.

Here's a pre-game routine you can try:

Night Before the Game
- Get Enough Sleep: Aim for 8-10 hours of quality sleep.
- Hydrate: Start hydrating the night before with plenty of water.
- Nutrition: Eat a balanced dinner with carbohydrates, proteins, and vegetables.

Morning of the Game

- Healthy Breakfast: Eat a nutritious breakfast 3-4 hours before the game. Include complex carbs (oatmeal, whole grain toast), protein (eggs, yogurt), and fruits.
- Hydration: Continue drinking water throughout the morning.

Arrival at the Field (1-1.5 Hours Before the Game)
- Check Gear: Ensure all equipment is in good condition – cleats, shin guards, uniform, and water bottle.
- Mental Preparation:
    - Listen to motivational music or engage in positive self-talk.
    - Visualize successful plays and scenarios during the game.

Warm-Up (45-60 Minutes Before the Game)
- Dynamic Stretching (10-15 minutes):
- Arm circles, leg swings, hip circles.
- Light Jogging (5-10 minutes):
- Gradually increase intensity to get the blood flowing.
- Drills and Skills (15-20 minutes):
- Passing drills, dribbling exercises, shooting practice.
- Team Strategy
- Discuss game plan, positions, and strategies with the coach and teammates.

Mental Focus (10-15 Minutes Before the Game)
- Team Huddle: Discuss team goals, encourage each other, and build team spirit.

- Individual Focus:
    - Take a few moments to breathe deeply and focus on personal goals for the game.
    - Remind yourself of key techniques and strategies.

Final Preparations (5 Minutes Before the Game)
- Last Hydration: Drink a small amount of water or a sports drink.
- Quick Gear Check: Ensure shoelaces are tied properly and shin guards are secure.
- Positive Mindset: Step onto the field with confidence and a positive attitude.

Importance of a Pre-game Routine
- **Consistency:** Having a routine ensures that you consistently prepare the same way, creating a sense of familiarity and comfort.
- **Focus:** A structured routine helps you focus on the task at hand, reducing distractions and pre-game jitters.
- **Physical Readiness:** Proper warm-ups reduce the risk of injury and ensure that muscles are ready for the physical demands of the game.
- **Mental Preparation:** Visualization and positive self-talk boost confidence and mental resilience.
- **Team Cohesion:** Pre-game huddles and discussions enhance team unity and communication.

By incorporating these steps into a pre-game routine, you can create a solid foundation for optimal performance and enjoyment of the game.

MY SOCCER JOURNAL

DATE   /   /

My Pregame Routine:

Postgame Reflection:

DATE   /   /

My Pregame Routine:

POSTGAME REFLECTION:

DATE   /   /

MY PREGAME ROUTINE:

POSTGAME REFLECTION:

DATE   /   /

My Pregame Routine:

POSTGAME REFLECTION:

DATE   /   /

My Pregame Routine:

Postgame Reflection:

DATE   /   /

My Pregame Routine:

POSTGAME REFLECTION:

DATE   /   /

My Pregame Routine:

Postgame Reflection:

DATE   /   /

My Pregame Routine:

POSTGAME REFLECTION:

DATE   /   /

MY PREGAME ROUTINE:

POSTGAME REFLECTION:

DATE   /   /

My Pregame Routine:

Postgame Reflection:

DATE   /   /

My Pregame Routine:

Postgame Reflection:

149

DATE   /   /

My Pregame Routine:

Postgame Reflection:

DATE   /   /

MY PREGAME ROUTINE:

POSTGAME REFLECTION:

DATE   /   /

My Pregame Routine:

POSTGAME REFLECTION:

DATE   /   /

My Pregame Routine:

Postgame Reflection:

DATE   /   /

My Pregame Routine:

POSTGAME REFLECTION:

DATE   /   /

My Pregame Routine:

Postgame Reflection:

DATE   /   /

MY PREGAME ROUTINE:

POSTGAME REFLECTION:

DATE   /   /

My Pregame Routine:

Postgame Reflection:

DATE   /   /

My Pregame Routine:

Postgame Reflection:

DATE   /   /

MY PREGAME ROUTINE:

POSTGAME REFLECTION:

DATE   /   /

My Pregame Routine:

Postgame Reflection:

DATE   /   /

My Pregame Routine:

Postgame Reflection:

DATE   /   /

My Pregame Routine:

Postgame Reflection:

162

DATE   /   /

My Pregame Routine:

Postgame Reflection:

DATE   /   /

My Pregame Routine:

Postgame Reflection:

DATE   /   /

My Pregame Routine:

Postgame Reflection:

DATE   /   /

My Pregame Routine:

POSTGAME REFLECTION:

DATE   /   /

My Pregame Routine:

Postgame Reflection:

DATE   /   /

My Pregame Routine:

Postgame Reflection:

DATE   /   /

My Pregame Routine:

Postgame Reflection:

DATE   /   /

My Pregame Routine:

POSTGAME REFLECTION:

DATE   /   /

MY PREGAME ROUTINE:

POSTGAME REFLECTION:

DATE   /   /

My Pregame Routine:

Postgame Reflection:

DATE   /   /

MY PREGAME ROUTINE:

POSTGAME REFLECTION:

DATE   /   /

My Pregame Routine:

POSTGAME REFLECTION:

DATE   /   /

My Pregame Routine:

Postgame Reflection:

DATE   /   /

My Pregame Routine:

POSTGAME REFLECTION:

DATE   /   /

My Pregame Routine:

Postgame Reflection:

DATE   /   /

My Pregame Routine:

POSTGAME REFLECTION:

DATE   /   /

MY PREGAME ROUTINE:

POSTGAME REFLECTION:

DATE   /   /

My Pregame Routine:

POSTGAME REFLECTION:

DATE / /

My Pregame Routine:

Postgame Reflection:

DATE   /   /

My Pregame Routine:

Postgame Reflection:

DATE   /   /

My Pregame Routine:

Postgame Reflection:

DATE   /   /

My Pregame Routine:

POSTGAME REFLECTION:

DATE   /   /

My Pregame Routine:

Postgame Reflection:

About the Author

Maria C. Bruce is a licensed psychotherapist and former medical doctor dedicated to empowering young athletes to reach their fullest potential. With her unique blend of expertise and personal experience as a dedicated parent to a son passionate about soccer, Maria has crafted a transformative guide tailored specifically for pre-teens and teens aiming to excel on the soccer field.

Maria's practical approach to sports psychology is informed by her work with Olympic and professional athletes, alongside her specialized training in positive cognitive-behavioral therapy, and optimal performance coaching.

Maria is also an emotional health expert contributor of popular publications, including Forbes, Cosmopolitan, Glamour, Medium, Vogue, and Vice.

Made in United States
Troutdale, OR
12/17/2024

26619211R10108